STARK

LEKTÜRE ENGLISCH

Alan Cartmell

The Adventures of Larry Lemming

für die Unterstufe

STARK

Umschlagbild: Rainer Thiele

ISBN: 978-3-89449-459-9

D-85318 Freising · Postfach 1852 · Tel. (0 81 61) 1790
Auflage 2008

Inhalt

Autor: Alan Cartmell
Illustrator: Rainer Thiele

Vorwort

Liebe Schülerinnen, liebe Schüler,

Als der Platz im heimatlichen Nest zu eng wird, macht sich Larry Lemming auf eine lange Reise. Auf seinem Weg zum großen Fluss begegnet er vielen Tieren und erlebt spannende Abenteuer.
Warum begleitet ihr Larry nicht auf seinem Weg und lernt mit ihm die Bewohner Alaskas kennen?
Die Geschichte ist in einfacher Sprache geschrieben und damit euch das Lesen leichter fällt, habe ich schwierige Wörter in der deutschen Übersetzung angegeben.

Ich wünsche euch viel Spaß bei eurer Reise!

Alan Cartmell

Chapter 1
Larry and his family

Larry was born on a fine morning in early spring. He was born in a nice warm nest his parents had made. The nest was in a burrow under the ground. Larry had two brothers and three sisters. The boys' names were Lumpy and Limpy and the girls' names were Lucy, Linda and Lorna.

Some days later Larry asked his mother: "When can we go out into the world?"

"Tomorrow," replied Mother, "but look after your brothers and sisters. Don't let them go far from the burrow[1] – there are many dangers in the world for us lemmings. If you see a black shadow[2] run as fast as you can back home."

***

So, late afternoon the next day, Larry, Lumpy, Limpy, Lucy, Linda and Lorna peeped out of the burrow. Then, for the first time, they saw the big wide world. There was still some snow on the ground, but, in the evening sunshine, Larry played hide-and-seek with his brothers and sisters in the grass near the burrow. Every time

1 *burrow* – Bau (von Tieren)
2 *shadow* – Schatten

Larry found one of his sisters they squeaked with delight[3]. Limpy and Lumpy slid[4], like little furry balls, down a small hill of snow and then climbed up again.

Suddenly it became dark. Larry remembered his mother's warning. "Quick," he shouted, "back home to the nest – it's the black shadow!"

***

When they were all back in the nest Larry said: "We saw the black shadow and quickly ran back home."

---

3 *delight* – Freude
4 *to slide, slid, slid* – rutschen

Mother Lemming carefully counted all her children: "Larry, Lucy, Lumpy, Lorna, Limpy and Linda. You are all here my dears. You were right to give warning, Larry, but what you saw was not the black shadow. It was just a big, dark cloud crossing the sun."

Then she sang them to sleep with a lemming lullaby[5].

"Sleep now, my dear little lemmings,
Safe in your nest nice and warm,
Sleep now, my cute little darlings,
Away from the snow and the storm."

5 *lullaby* – Schlaflied

Chapter 2
Larry's farewell

After a few weeks Larry, Lumpy, Lorna, Lucy, Limpy and Linda had grown so big that Father Lemming said: "The nest is too small for all you fat young lemmings. It's time for some of you to leave the nest.

"I want to see the big wide world," said Larry.

"Well, you are the fattest and strongest of our children," said Father, "so you can be the first to go."

He thought for a few moments and then said: "When some of us lemmings leave the nest we always travel down into the valley. Then we go west to a very big wide river. A friend told me that there is a wonderful country for lemmings on the other side."

***

Mother Lemming looked very sad and a tear[1] ran down her cheek. "Take care of yourself in the big wide world, Larry," she whispered, "and always watch out for the black shadow."

That evening, Lucy, Linda, Limpy, Lumpy and Lorna all came out of the burrow to see him off. They all waved and sang:

---

1 *tear* – Träne

"Goodbye and good luck, dear Larry,
As you look for that river so wide,
And when you run down to the valley,
From all dangers be careful to hide."

"Don't worry," said Larry, "I can take care of myself[2]." And off he ran through the snow tracks towards the valley and the big wide river.

2 *to take care of oneself* – auf sich selbst aufpassen

Chapter 3
Larry meets Dora Duck

Larry ran along the snow tunnels and tracks they had made playing around the nest. After a while he came to a stream[1] flowing down to the valley. "Is this the big wide river?" he said to himself. "No, it can't be, because I can see the other side."

Larry had never been swimming before and he put one paw carefully into the water. "Ugh, it's very cold," he said aloud.

Just then a strange animal with a brown head, yellow beak and white body came swimming along.

***

"Who are you?" said Larry.

"Quack, quack," she replied, "my name is Dora and I'm a duck. I live on the farm over there. And who are you?"

"I'm Larry Lemming," he said proudly, "and I'm going down to the valley and the big wide river."

"Well, if the water is too cold, you can get on my back and I'll paddle you across. Quack, quack, it's not far."

---

1 *stream* – Bach

So Larry jumped on Dora's back and she paddled carefully to the other side. Larry jumped off and said: "Thank you very much, Dora, and now can I ask you a question?"

"Of course," said Dora as she waddled onto the bank.

"My mother warned me about the black shadow. Do you know what it is?" asked Larry.

"Quack, quack, no," she replied, "but my mother warned me about a big red animal with a bushy tail. So watch out for it, too!"

"Goodbye, and thanks again," called out Larry as he ran towards the bushes near the edge[2] of the forest.

***

Behind a bush two bright yellow eyes were watching Larry. Freddy Fox licked his lips and curled his bushy red tail over his brown legs. "Here comes my supper," he thought.

2 *edge* – Rand

Chapter 4
Larry and the red fox

The sun was setting now and Larry thought: “I must soon find a place to sleep. I’ll miss the warm nest and my brothers and sisters.”

He ran in and out of the trees looking for a small hole where he could sleep. He was happily singing a little lemming song.

“Running here and running there,
We live our lives without a care.”

And so he didn’t hear Freddy the Fox quietly following him. Every time Larry came to a tree, he stopped and looked for a hole under it. Every time he stopped, Freddy the red fox came nearer and nearer.

***

It was almost dark now and the moon was beginning to shine through the trees. Larry stopped singing. Was that a noise he heard in the bushes behind him? He stood up and his little whiskers[1] twitched as he sniffed the wind. What was that strange smell?

“Hello, little lemming,” said a voice from behind a tree, “don’t be afraid of Freddy Fox.”

---

1 *whiskers* – Barthaare

Then he saw a bushy tail and Larry remembered Dora Duck's warning. He ran as fast as his little legs could carry him. He heard the snap of teeth behind him as he ran toward a big old beech tree[2]. He stopped at the tree, breathless[3]. He was trapped. He turned round and the shape[4] of Freddy the red fox covered the moon.

"Quick, in here," said a soft voice near him.

Larry looked and saw a dark hole under a root of the tree. He jumped into it and the soft voice said:

"Quick, quick, my dear little fellow,
Run behind me as fast as you can.
My tail is what you must follow;
Away from the fox we must run."

---

2 *beech tree* – Buche
3 *breathless* – außer Atem
4 *shape* – Gestalt

Chapter 5
Larry and the rabbits

When Larry jumped into the hole, all he could see in front of him, was a round white tail. They ran along small passages and sometimes they turned left and sometimes they turned right. Then, suddenly, they came to a bigger hole, deep under the ground.

"You're safe now, little animal. Freddy the red fox can't come down here – the passages are too small," said the soft furry[1] animal with the white tail.

"Oh, thank you," said Larry, "but who are you?"

"My name is Robbie. I'm a rabbit," he replied, "and this is Mrs Rita Rabbit. These are our four children – Rosie, Ricky, Ronny and Rolly. And what's your name, little animal?"

"Hello," said Larry to the children, "I'm Larry Lemming. I'm going to see the world. I'm on my way down to the valley and then to the big wide river. Is it far?"

"I don't know," replied Robbie. Our world is around the tree. Sometimes we go down to the farmer's field. In summer he grows nice tasty, green lettuces there."

"Yes, we love the farmer's nice green leaves[2]," called out the rabbit children.

---

1 *furry* – pelzig
2 *leaves* – Blätter

"Now off to bed, you children," said Mrs Rita Rabbit.

"Oh, please tell us a bedtime story first, Dad," cried Rosie, Ricky, Ronnie and Rolly.

"Tell us the story about the eggs and our grandfather Romany Rabbit. We all like that story."

***

Larry Lemming sat down with the rabbit children in the warm nest and they all got ready to listen.

Chapter 6
The story of the first Easter eggs

When Rosie, Ricky, Ronny, Rolly Rabbit and Larry Lemming were all sitting quietly in the nest, Father Rabbit began:

"Once upon a time[1], many, many years ago, all the animals on the big farm down in the valley met in the barn. Harry the Horse said: 'Sally and Peter are such nice children. They always help on the farm and often give us our food when their father is not at home. Let's think of a nice present to give them for Easter.'

'Good idea,' all the other animals cried.

'I know,' said Cocky the cockerel[2], 'I'll get all my hens to lay eggs and we can hide them around the farm for Peter and Sally to find.' All the other animals thought it was a good idea, too: Carrie the Cow, Harry the Horse, Porky the Pig, Lilian the Lamb and Dougie the Dog. So all the hens worked hard before Easter and laid lots of eggs. All the animals helped to hide the eggs in different places: in the barn, behind the cow-shed, in the stable[3], and even under the haystack[4]. Sally and Peter, of course, always found the eggs, but, because

---

1 *once upon a time* – es war einmal
2 *cockerel* – Hahn
3 *stable* – Pferdestall
4 *haystack* – Heuhaufen

they were only white, they didn't know they were an Easter present.

And so the animals were very disappointed.

One year, however, Cocky the Cockerel said: 'If the eggs were different colours like my beautiful long tail, the children would know the eggs were a special present.'

'But how can we do that,' cried all the other animals.

'That's easy,' said Cocky, 'we just need an artist[5] to paint them.'

'I think I know the right person,' cried Lilian the Lamb, 'Romany Rabbit. He is an artist and I often see him near the wood. I'll ask him.'

***

So, a few days later, Lilian the Lamb met Romany Rabbit and told him about the problem.

'Well,' said Romany Rabbit:

> 'I'm the jolly rabbit painter,
> I paint all colours true
> Give me your eggs at Easter,
> And I'll paint them all for you.'

'I'll paint the eggs in beautiful colours,' he continued. 'Then I'll come and hide them around the farmyard for you.'

---

5 *artist* – Künstler

When Lilian the Lamb told the other animals, they were very pleased.[6]

'I hope he uses some of the colours that are in my beautiful long tail,' called out Cocky the Cockerel.

So every year, from that time, Romany Rabbit and his sons, his grandsons and great-grandsons have always painted the chickens' eggs in beautiful colours and hidden them around the farm. Sally and Peter, like all children, always find every egg and know that they are a special present for Easter."

***

Robbie Rabbit looked down at his children, but Rosie, Ricky, Ronny, Rolly, and Larry Lemming too, were already fast[7] asleep.

6 *to be pleased* – erfreut sein
7 *fast* – hier: tief

Chapter 7
Larry meets Gracie the grey squirrel

Very early the next morning, Robbie Rabbit woke Larry Lemming and said: "It's safe now. Freddy the red fox has gone home to sleep."

He led Larry along the passage to another hole under a tree. "Go now, young Larry and good luck on your journey to the big wide river," said Robbie.

"Thanks again," called out Larry and he quickly ran through the trees.

***

He was very hungry now and started looking for something to eat. Suddenly he saw a grey animal with a bushy tail jump from a tree to the ground. Larry remembered[1] the red fox, the other animal with a bushy tail, and quickly hid under some leaves. He watched as the animal hopped about among the bushes scratching the ground. Then under some old leaves it uncovered some nuts. Larry was so hungry now he crept towards the grey animal. When the animal saw him it quickly jumped back onto the tree.

"Who are you," it cried, "and what do you want?"

---

1 *to remember* – sich erinnern

Larry saw that the grey animal was not a fox after all and said:

"I'm Larry Lemming on my way west to the big wide river. I'm also very hungry. Could I have some of your nuts?" The grey animal came down the tree and said,

"I'm Gracie the grey squirrel.
I climb the highest fir trees,
And jump from branch to branch,
I'm looking for the nut seeds,
I hide for my spring lunch."

Then she said: "I carefully hid[2] these nuts last autumn, but you can have some if you are very hungry."

"Oh, thank you," said Larry and they both had a good nut breakfast.

When they had finished breakfast, Larry asked Gracie: "Is it far to the big wide river?"

---

2 *to hide, hid, hidden* – verstecken

"I don't know," she replied, "I never leave the forest, but I'll climb to the top[3] of this high tree and look for you." Gracie jumped onto the tree and Larry watched as[4] she went round and round and higher and higher. After a few minutes she came down again and said, "I can't see a big wide river but, in the west, I can see big hills with white tops. Perhaps the big wide river is on the other side."

"Thank you very much. I'll be on my way now," said Larry, and he ran on once more, towards the big hills with the white tops.

---

3 *top (of a tree)* – Wipfel
4 *as* – als

Chapter 8
Paul and Michaela's bridge

The big hills with white tops that Gracie had seen from the top of her tree were, of course[1], mountains with snow on them. In these mountains was a hut made of wood. In the summer Jim, his wife Sarah and their two children, Michaela and Paul, lived there. Jim was a farmer and he took his cows up to the higher meadows for the summer months. The meadows were filled with long grass and beautiful yellow, pink and blue flowers. Paul and Michaela loved playing in the meadows. Sometimes Paul and his father fished for trout[2] in the mountain stream.

***

One fine spring morning Paul said: "Let's play in the meadow on the other side of the stream."

"But the stream is much too fast and cold to swim," said Michaela.

"There's some wood under our hut. We'll make a wooden bridge," answered Paul.

They carried two long pieces of wood and carefully made a bridge across the stream. Michaela was nervous

---

1 *of course* – natürlich
2 *trout* – Forelle

at first, but Paul crossed over and showed her it was safe. Then they played in the meadows[3] right up to the edge of the forest. Michaela was happily singing her meadow song:

"I love playing in our meadows,
Among the cows and sheep,
But best of all, I love the flowers,
That grow beside our stream."

They picked lots of those beautiful wild flowers to take home to mother. When the sun began to go down, they went back home to a nice supper of tea, brown bread, butter and home-made strawberry jam.

***

While Michaela and Paul were playing in the meadow, Larry Lemming was running towards the snowy mountains. "I hope there aren't any black shadows there," he thought. It was evening now and he was running happily through a meadow with beautiful yellow, pink and blue flowers. Suddenly he came to a stream. "Well, let's see if I can swim," he said and dived into the stream. Before he could swim one stroke, he was swept[4] under the water. Gasping for breath[5], he got hold of a rock some way down stream. "That was a lucky escape," he thought as he crawled out of the

---

3 *meadow* – Wiese
4 *to sweep, swept, swept* – (weg)spülen
5 *to gasp for breath* – nach Luft schnappen

water, "but how do I cross the stream?" Then he saw it: Michaela and Paul's wooden bridge.

Michaela and Paul didn't know, of course, that they had helped little Larry Lemming go on his way to the big wide river. They were just enjoying their supper of brown bread, butter and strawberry jam.

Chapter 9
Larry hears a reindeer story

When Larry had crossed the wooden bridge, he ran on towards the setting sun[1]. He was hungry after his swim in the fast stream and soon found some pine cones[2] at the edge of the forest. After he had eaten them, he ran on until he came to the white stuff that Gracie had seen from her tree. He pushed his face into it. "It's only snow," he said to himself. "It's the same stuff as at home." "Atischoo," he sneezed[3] and the snow on his whiskers flew off. Then he ran on quickly along the edge of the forest, in the snow tracks that other animals had made.

***

Suddenly he heard heavy footsteps in front of him. He saw two very big animals coming towards him, and so he hid underneath[4] an old log. One of the animals had big things growing on its head.

---

1 *setting sun* – untergehende Sonne
2 *pine cone* – Kiefernzapfen
3 *to sneeze* – niesen
4 *underneath* – unter

It was a Mother Caribou and her baby. They came right up to the log[5] where Larry was hiding and lay down.

"Perhaps this animal with things growing on its head is the black shadow," Larry thought. "I must be careful."

After a while Baby Caribou said: "Before we go to sleep, please tell me a story."

"I'll tell you about your uncle," its mother began.

***

"His name is Rudolf and he is one of the biggest and strongest reindeer in the forest. Your uncle's antlers[6]

5 *log* – Holzklotz
6 *antlers* – Geweih

are admired[7] by everyone. At this moment he is probably[8] travelling north to meet Father Christmas again. Every year six of the strongest reindeer help pull Father Christmas in his sleigh. Your Uncle Rudolf was very proud when Father Christmas chose him last year."

"What does Father Christmas do?" asked Baby Caribou.

"Well," said Mother, "in early December all the children ask Father Christmas to bring them a present on Christmas day. He collects all the presents, puts them in bags, and then puts them on his big sleigh[9]. Then on Christmas Eve[10], Uncle Rudolf and the other reindeer pull Father Christmas through the sky to each house. Father Christmas then climbs down the chimney and puts the presents under the Christmas tree. All the children want to have the presents on Christmas morning, so it's very hard work."

"I hope when I grow up[11] Father Christmas will let me pull the big sleigh, too," said Baby Caribou.

***

---

7 *to admire* – bewundern
8 *probably* – wahrscheinlich
9 *sleigh* – Schlitten
10 *Christmas Eve* – Tag <u>vor</u> Weihnachten (Heilig Abend)
11 *to grow up* – erwachsen werden

Then before they went to sleep Mother Caribou clopped[12] with a front hoof[13] the beat of the caribou song:

"In spring we start our journeys,
From south to north we go.
Look, see our high held antlers,
As we wander through the snow."

"They are big, but friendly animals," Larry thought, "I can sleep safely near them." And soon, from under the log, came the soft 'sszzzz' noise of Lemmy snoring[14].

12 *to clop* – schlagen, klopfen
13 *front hoof* – Vorderhuf
14 *to snore* – schnarchen

Chapter 10
Gerda the snow goose

The next morning, before Mother and Baby Caribou were awake, Larry was running down the other side of the mountain. He was enjoying the snow. Every time he came to a little hill of it, he jumped onto it and slid down. "Wheee, this is great fun," he shouted.

After one long downhill slide he suddenly bumped into something.

"Watch where you're going, you clumsy[1] little mouse," said a voice.

"I'm not a mouse," said Larry, "I'm Larry Lemming. Who are you? I can't see you."

"Right in front of your nose," said the voice, and then Larry saw a head and beak[2] above lots of snow-white feathers.

"My name is Gerda. I'm a snow goose," she said. "I was just going with my goslings[3] for our morning swim. You frightened them when you bumped into me. They are all here under my wings[4]." And Larry saw six little yellow beaks peeping out from under the white feathers.

---

1 *clumsy* – ungeschickt
2 *beak* – Schnabel
3 *gosling* – Gänseküken
4 *wing* – Flügel

"I'm on my way west to the big wide river," said Larry, "Is it far[5]?"

"Well, you can come down to the water with us and look," said Gerda. Larry followed Gerda and the six snow-white goslings as they waddled[6] down to the water. Just as they got to[7] the water a black shadow came across the morning sun. All the goslings dashed under Gerda's wings – Larry Lemming, too!

***

A moment later there was a splash[8] and Gerda said: "It's okay, my little ones, don't be frightened. Your

5 *far* – weit
6 *to waddle* – watscheln
7 *to get to* – ankommen
8 *splash* – Spritzer

father Gunter Gander has come to see you." Gunter Gander paddled over and his children swam to meet him.

"Who is that peeping from under your wing, Gerda?" he asked.

"Oh," said Gerda, "let me introduce[9] Larry Lemming. Larry is going west to the big wide river." Larry slowly came out and said: "I thought you were the black shadow my mother warned me about."

"You are right to watch out, my young lemming; I tell my gosling to be careful, too," said Father Gunter Gander.

"Can you swim?" Gerda asked Larry.

"Well, I've only tried[10] once and the water was too fast and cold for me," replied Larry.

"Well, now is your chance to try again," said Gunter Gander. So Larry bravely[11] dashed into the water.

"Yes," he said, "I can swim. So good-bye you little goslings, I'm off to the other side."

As he swam, Larry started singing a little lemming tune again:

"I am swimming, I am swimming,
Look! Watch me take a dive,
It's just the same as running.
To reach the other side."

---

9 *to introduce* –vorstellen
10 *to try, tried, tried* – versuchen
11 *brave* – tapfer

Chapter 11
Larry and the two fishermen

Larry soon found he was quite a strong swimmer and sometimes he dived[1] under the water. He saw lots of green plants waving[2] there. Now and again he saw big fish with speckled[3] sides swimming between the plants.

After a short while he came to the bank on the opposite side. "This can't be the big wide river Father told me about," Larry thought, "I crossed it too quickly." He lay in the warm sun to let his coat and whiskers dry. Then he started running along the bank again. Suddenly, he heard the loud splash of water. The sound was coming from a waterfall, and he watched big silver fish jumping high in the air. Sometimes they fell back and had to try again, but usually they landed in the higher water and swam swiftly on.

And as they swam they sang:

"I love the clear fresh waters,
When I'm salty from the sea,
And leaping[4] up the waterfalls,
Is the greatest fun for me."

---

1 *to dive* – tauchen
2 *to wave* – winken
3 *speckled* – gesprenkelt, mit Punkten
4 *to leap* – springen

A little later Larry heard a voice shout: "I've got one!" He hurried quickly under a bush and peeped out. He saw a man with a long stick in his hand. The stick was bending[5] over the water.

Then he saw one of the big silver fish jump out of the water near the man. Another man came with a big net[6] and Larry saw that the big silver fish was caught on a line[7]. The other man put the net in the water and lifted out the big silver fish.

"It must weigh at least[8] ten kilos," said the man with the fishing rod. "It'll make a nice supper for us tonight."

"Yes," said his friend, "we'll have salmon[9] steaks barbecued over the fire."

---

5 *to bend* – sich biegen
6 *net* – Netz
7 *caught on a line* – gefangen an einer Schnur
8 *at least* – wenigstens
9 *salmon* – Lachs

***

Larry was frightened. He didn't want to be caught in the big net, too. He waited until the men had gone to barbecue their salmon before he looked for his own supper. Then he ran on quickly until he came to a big field of young sweet corn[10]. "Yum, yum," he thought as he dived between the stalks, "this is food for me!"

---

10 *corn*– Mais

Chapter 12
Larry meets a strange animal

Larry ran into the field of young sweet corn and started to nibble the bottom of one of the stalks[1]. He knew that when he had nibbled it through, it would fall down and he could then eat the juicy sweet corn cob. He was just starting on his first stalk when a snuffly[2] voice cried, "Stop that. What do you think you are doing?" Larry looked around but could see no one.

***

"Behind you, you silly rat[3]," said the voice. Larry turned round and saw, between the stalks, two small black eyes looking at him. Under the eyes was a black nose with whiskers. On its back were lots of long spikes sticking up.

"I'm not a rat," said Larry, "I'm Larry Lemming. Who are you?"

The animal clapped its paws[4] and sang:

"My name is Patty Porcupine,
My spines are very long,

1 *stalk* – Stängel
2 *snuffly* – schniefend
3 *rat* – Ratte
4 *paws* – Pfoten

They rattle when I'm feeling fine,
And when I sing my song."

"I'm a porcupine[5] and if you nibble that stalk it will fall down and the corn cob[6] will stick on my spines[7]."
"Oh, sorry, Patty Porcupine," said Larry, "there are enough other stalks to nibble."
He started to move away, but then she said: "Well, now you are here, you can stay for a chat[8]. Where are you from, Larry Lemming, and where are you going?"

"I have come from the other side of the big hills with snow on them. We were six in my family. When we all got too big for our nest, my father told me to go west and look for the big wide river. Have you seen it Patty Porcupine?"

"No," she replied, "I can't see very far."

"I have had a lot of adventures on my journey, too," said Larry. "I was nearly eaten by a fox and I almost

---

5 *porcupine* – Stachelschwein
6 *corn cob* – Maiskolben
7 *spine* – Stachel
8 *chat* – Schwätzchen

drowned[9] in a fast and cold river. Gunter Gander also made me dash for cover when he flew over. I thought he was the black shadow my mother warned me about. Do you know what the black shadow is, Patty Porcupine?"

"Well," she replied, "when I was very young I always played hide-and-seek with my little brother Peter. Then one day, while we were playing, we saw a black shadow. I put my head under my body and stuck out all my little spines. But, when I peeped out[10] again my brother Peter was gone, and I never saw him again."

"That is a sad story, Patty Porcupine – I hope you tell your own children to be careful!"

***

It was almost dark now and Larry said good-bye to Patty. "Safe journey, Larry," she called out and rattled[11] her spines, as he dashed off towards the wood near the cornfield.

---

9 *to drown* – ertrinken
10 *to peep out* – hervor blinzeln
11 *to rattle* – rasseln

Chapter 13
Larry meets a story teller

Larry went very carefully into the forest. He still remembered the red fox. The floor of this wood was very soft. Under the trees were very thin leaves, like needles. There were also some pine cones which Larry thought would be nice for breakfast. Then he made a little nest in the pine needles and started to sleep.

Suddenly he was wide awake[1]. He had heard a funny noise from a tree near him.

"Twit, twoo, twit, twoo," called a loud voice. He looked up and saw a strange bird sitting in a tree. It had white feathers[2], big round eyes and little ears.

"Twit twoo, twit twoo, come hear my cry.
Twit twoo, twit twoo, before I fly,
Twit twoo, twit twoo, come gather round,
And listen to a wise bird's sound."

"Twit, twoo," said the snowy owl, "who wants to hear a story?"

***

1 *wide awake* – hellwach
2 *feather* – Feder

Slowly a few animals came to the bottom of the tree. Larry could see a rabbit, a squirrel, a little deer and also another lemming. "Wait for me, Olly Owl," said a muffled voice. Then a small hill of earth pushed out of the ground and a little animal with a pointed nose[3], very small eyes, and big strong forepaws[4] popped out.

"Good evening, Molly Mole[5]," said the other animals.

"What story have you got for us tonight?" called out the squirrel.

"Well, first tell me the names of some of the trees in the forest," said Olly Owl.

3 *pointed nose* – spitz zulaufende Nase
4 *forepaws* – Vorderpfoten
5 *mole* – Maulwurf

"The birch tree[6]," called the young deer, "I like eating the leaves."

"The oak tree[7]," said the squirrel, "I like eating the acorns."

The willow tree[8]," called Molly Mole. "Lovely worms[9] grow under it."

"The beech tree," called the rabbit, "I can make nice burrows in between the roots."

"Twit-twoo. Very good," said Olly Owl, "but my story tonight will be about a very special tree. So listen carefully." And all the animals sat quietly around the tree waiting for the story to begin.

---

6 *birch tree* – Birke
7 *oak tree* – Eiche
8 *willow tree* – Weide
9 *worm* – Wurm

Chapter 14
Larry hears the tree story

"Well," said Olly Owl, "twit, twoo, if you are all comfortable, I'll tell you the story of a tree in this forest and how it became the first Christmas tree.

Then he started his story:

***

"It was a December night a long, long time ago. The snow was deep and it was very cold. Father Christmas, however[1], was busy putting all the children's presents into his sleigh. The reindeer were all standing ready to pull it across the sky. Iolanthe, the fairy[2], was helping him put the parcels into the sleigh.

Suddenly Father Christmas said to her: 'What the children need is somewhere special to put their presents. When I go down the chimney and into the room, I don't know where to put them. Sometimes I put them on the table, or on a chair and sometimes just in a stocking. Have you got any ideas, Iolanthe?'

'Well,' said Iolanthe, who was the fairy of the forest, 'a small tree would be nice. You could put the presents under it.'

---

1 *however* – jedoch
2 *fairy* – Fee

'What a good idea,' said Father Christmas, 'go quickly into the forest and bring me some trees.' So Iolanthe went into the forest and collected five different trees: a willow tree, a birch tree, an oak tree, a fir tree and a beech tree. Father Christmas looked at the birch tree. 'No,' he said, 'this tree is not strong enough[3].' He looked at the oak tree. 'No,' he said, 'this tree's bark[4] is too rough.' He looked at the willow tree. 'No,' he said, 'this tree's branches[5] are too thin.' He looked at the beech tree. 'No,' he said, 'this tree has all its old brown leaves.' Then he picked up the fir tree. 'This little tree is just right for presents. It is strong, it has a sweet smell and nice fresh, green, needles in the winter. I'll use[6] this one. Thank you, little Iolanthe. What is the name of this tree?' he asked her.

'It's called a fir tree,' she replied.

'Well,' said Father Christmas, 'from now on it will be known as the Christmas tree.'

Iolanthe was so happy, she sang:

'I am the forest Fairy,
Iolanthe is my name,
You may see me faintly[7],
Dancing like a flame.'

Father Christmas was pleased, too. And so that year Father Christmas took small fir trees on the sleigh with

---

3 *enough* – genug
4 *bark* – Rinde
5 *branch* – Ast
6 *to use* – benützen
7 *faint* – schwach

him. In every house he put the tree in the corner of the room and put the presents under it.

On Christmas morning, all fathers and mothers saw that it was a good idea. And, since then[9], every Christmas, they have put their own fir trees in the living room and decorated them. Father Christmas and Iolanthe are always very happy now, when they see the nice fir Christmas trees with their beautiful shining candles and pretty glass balls[10]."

***

"That was a nice story," all the animals cried. "Thank you."

9 *since then* – seit damals
10 *glass balls* – Glaskugeln

Twit, twoo," answered Olly Owl turning his head round and round.

"Now all you little animals go to bed," cried the squirrel, "before Olly Owl looks for his supper."

Chapter 15
Larry and the bright lights

After Olly Owl had finished the story, Larry said to the other lemming: "Hello, my name is Larry. What's your name and where are you going?"

"I'm Lotty Lemming," she replied, "I'm going west to the big wide river. My father told me there is a big happy land on the other side with plenty[1] of room and food for all lemmings. I've come with some friends."

"I'm going there, too," said Larry. "Well, come and meet my friends. You can travel with us," said Lotty. So Larry met all Lotty's friends. He told them about his adventures with Freddy Fox, Robbie Rabbit, Dora Duck, and all the other animals. They told him about their adventures, too.

***

While they were swapping[2] stories the night sky suddenly became very bright. "It's too early for morning," cried Larry, "what is happening?" They all watched as the sky became filled with bright colours. They were moving about the sky like beautiful big curtains. They changed from red to yellow, then to blue

1 *plenty* – massenhaft, viel
2 *to swap* – austauschen

and then back to red again. "I'm frightened[3]," whispered Lotty. Larry looked and saw she was a beautiful young lady lemming. She had covered her eyes with her paws.

"Don't worry, Lotty," said Larry, "they are only pretty lights – they won't[4] hurt you." The lemmings couldn't hear, but high above them the lights sang:

"Can you see our colours shining,
All through the darkest nights?
And how we keep on changing,
Our lovely magic lights?"

***

Just then a furry[5] animal with black and white stripes on its tail came snuffling along. "Hello," cried Larry, "who are you?"

"Who wants to know?" said a grumpy[6] voice.

"We are lemmings going west to the big wide river, and my name is Larry Lemming," answered Larry.

"Do you know what these beautiful lights in the sky mean[7]?" asked Lotty.

"I'm Roddy Raccoon and I'm not a scientist," he replied. "But so that you'll get out of my way, I'll tell

---

3 *to be frightened* – Angst haben
4 *won't* – werden nicht
5 *furry* – pelzig
6 *grumpy* – grantig
7 *to mean* – bedeuten

you. They are the northern lights[8] and they come every year. I haven't got time, however, to stand and look at pretty lights – I've got my family to feed. So, if you don't mind, I'll be on my way. Goodbye."

Larry and the others watched Roddy Raccoon go down to the nearby stream.

They saw him catch a fish, wash it in the water and take it off to his family.

"What a miserable old animal," said Lotty. And all the little lemmings squeaked[9] with laughter as they ran higgledy-piggledy[10] among the soft pine needles. And above them the northern lights continued their wonderful show.

---

8 *northern lights* – Nordlicht
9 *to squeak* – quietschen
10 *higgledy-piggledy* – durcheinander

Chapter 16
Larry and the guns

The next day, before dawn, Lotty woke everyone up and said: “Come on you sleepy-heads, it’s time to get on our way.” Larry was still tired, however, and said: “You go on, I can catch you up[1].” Lotty was a bit disappointed[2] that Larry wasn’t coming too, but she ran off with the other lemmings.

Larry yawned[3], stretched and twitched his whiskers. “I’m a little thirsty,” he murmured, “after that late night watching the lights. I think I’ll find a stream and have a drink.” So he started running away from the forest and towards the fields. He enjoyed running through the grass with all the beautiful yellow and white flowers.

***

Then he came to a small brook in the field and had a nice drink. Suddenly he saw a hut and two men carrying long metal things under their arms. He remembered the two fishermen and their big net and was frightened. “I must hide,” he thought and ran

---

1 *to catch up* – einholen
2 *disappointed* – enttäuscht
3 *to yawn* – gähnen

away from the hut and hid in the grass. Suddenly one of the men shouted: "There he goes." And there was a very loud bang[4] and then another bang. "Missed him," shouted the other man. "He has escaped[5] again."

When he heard the big bangs, Larry was even more frightened and crept deeper under the long grass. Then he heard a thump[6] and a strange animal with long legs, very long ears and big brown eyes, landed beside him. When the animal saw him he panted[7]: "My, that was close, they nearly got me that time."

"Who are you?" whispered Larry.

"Harry Hare is my name, little animal," he whispered. "Those two men always try to shoot me, but with my long legs I'm too fast for them.

---

4 *bang* – Knall
5 *to escape* – entfliehen
6 *thump* – Bums
7 *to pant* – keuchen

"I like leaping over ditches[8],
I like jumping over streams,
In springtime you can see me,
Running through the fields."

When I've had a rest[9] I'll be off[10] again."

***

A moment later, without even saying goodbye, Harry suddenly jumped up and ran across the field, zig-zagging first this way and then the other. "I forgot to ask him the way down to the river," murmured Larry.

8 *ditch* – Graben
9 *rest* – (Verschnauf-)pause
10 *I'll be off* – werde ich weg sein

Chapter 17
Larry and the wolves

When Larry saw that Harry Hare wasn't going to come back, he started running towards the forest again. "I must find the other lemmings," he thought. He climbed onto a big rock[1], stood up on his back legs, twitched[2] his little whiskers, and sniffed the wind. The wind smelt colder and he saw that he was in a valley between the high snow-topped mountains.

When he reached the forest it was already dark and he searched under the trees for some tasty roots[3] to eat. While he was nibbling the roots he heard a strange noise. "Howooo, howooo" came from deep in the forest. And then the same noise came from another place: "howooo, howooo."

***

Larry crept quickly under a log and watched. He saw a grey animal much bigger than the red fox come into the clearing[4]. The animal suddenly threw back its head and

1 *rock* – Fels
2 *to twitch* – zwirbeln
3 *root* – Wurzel
4 *clearing* – Lichtung

howled once again: "Howooo, howooo." Slowly other grey animals came into the clearing, too.

Their eyes gleamed[5] yellow in the moonlight, as they all lay down.

"Well, that was a good day's hunting," said an old grey wolf. "I hope nobody is still hungry."

"No," all the others replied.

***

One of the young wolf cubs asked: "We hunt the other animals, does anyone hunt us?"

"A good question my boy," said another grey wolf. "We are kings of the forest, nobody hunts us. Listen to our song:

---

5 *to gleam* – leuchten

"The forest is our kingdom,
We rule it day and night.
We run and leap in freedom,
For hunting is our right.
Howooo. Howooo"

"You are wrong," said the old grey leader of the pack[6]. "We have only one enemy and that is the animal who stands on two legs and carries a gun. 'Man' he calls himself."

"Why does man hunt us?" asked another young cub. "Are we good to eat?"

"No," said the old grey wolf, "but he is always afraid of us. I don't know why, because many, many years ago when the world was very young, he was friends with us. He even took some of our young cubs[7] and trained them to help him. Man calls them 'dogs' now and many have strange shapes and sizes."

***

When he had finished speaking, all the wolves slowly settled down to sleep.

Larry crept quietly away from the wolves and thought: "I saw those men with the big net and men were hunting Harry Hare, too. I must watch out for man as well as the black shadow."

---

6 *pack* – Rudel
7 *cub* – Welpe (junger Hund/Wolf)

Chapter 18
The black shadow

The next morning Larry woke up early and ran out of the forest. He started looking for the other lemmings again. All day, he looked for them along the valley. "They can't be far away now," he thought. Then suddenly he heard squeaking noises coming from the other side of a small hill. "Those little friends of mine are making a lot of noise," he said, as he ran towards the sound. He soon found them and saw that they were all playing among[1] the rocks at the bottom of the mountain. Some were climbing up the rocks and then rolling off. Others were chasing each other around the plants[2] growing between the rocks. They were all noisily squeaking with laughter. "Come on, Larry," they called. "It's good fun." "Yes," cried Lotty, "come and play hide-and-seek[3] with us."

***

It was a beautiful evening. The sky was turning[4] red with only a few white clouds on the mountain tops. So

---

1 *among* – zwischen
2 *plant* – Pflanze
3 *to play hide-and-seek* – Verstecken spielen
4 *to turn* – sich ändern

Larry, too, climbed the rocks and tumbled down and played hide-and-seek among the plants.

Then it happened. Suddenly a big black shadow crossed the rocks where they were playing. "Run," shouted Larry. Larry and all the lemmings scattered[5] in every direction. There was a loud sound of beating wings and a pair of sharp talons grasped[6] at Larry. But Larry had dived right under a rock. He saw the sharp curved beak and yellow eyes looking for him. Then it was gone, and he heard the beating of wings again. He peeped out and saw a giant bird flying. As it flew away its feathers shone[7] in the evening sun. And ringing out across the valley, the frightened lemmings heard the golden eagle's song:

"I beat the air with my strong wings,
I watch the world with my keen eye,
I grasp my prey[8] with my sharp talons,
For I am the king of earth and sky."

---

5 *to scatter* – sich zerstreuen
6 *to grasp* – (er)greifen
7 *to shine, shone, shone* – leuchten
8 *prey* – *Beute*

The great golden eagle flew higher and higher until it disappeared[9] among the clouds on the mountain tops.

***

"Phew," gasped Larry, "so that was the black shadow. Mother was right to warn us." Slowly the little band of lemmings came out of hiding. They were all shaking with fear.

"Thanks to you, Larry, we all had a lucky escape. We must be more careful from now on," whispered Lotty.

---

9 *to disappear* – verschwinden

Chapter 19
Two more dangerous fishermen

After their terrible fright[1] with the black shadow, all the lemmings decided[2] to try to reach the big wide river as soon as possible. "It would be safer if we split up[3]," said Larry. So, one by one, they ran off in the direction of the setting sun.

While Larry was running along, he suddenly heard a splashing sound and he came to a fast stream full of rocks and noisy rough water. He also heard strange growling noises coming from the rocks. He remembered the fisherman's net and so crept very carefully towards the sound. And there he saw, on the rocks, two very large, furry animals.

***

At first, Larry thought they were thirsty and were drinking from the stream. But then he watched as the biggest animal suddenly dipped[4] its large paw into the water. The animal then quickly threw[5] a large silver

---

1 *fright* – Schrecken
2 *to decide* – sich entschließen
3 *to split up* – sich aufteilen
4 *to dip* – tauchen
5 *to throw, threw, thrown* – werfen

fish on to the bank. A few minutes later, the smaller animal caught one in its mouth.

Then Larry watched as the two grizzly bears had a good meal from the silver salmon.

"I hope this isn't the big wide river," thought Larry. "If those animals can catch fish so easily, they could catch me, and my lemming friends, while we are swimming across." Larry hid under a big rock away from the animals. After a while[6] the two grizzly bears came past[7] him, grunting and growling.

***

"That was a good evening's fishing," said Gerry the bigger grizzly bear.

---

6 *after a while* – nach einer Weile
7 *to come past* – vorbeikommen

"Yes," agreed Greta the smaller one, "let's hope we have a few more good days like today. Then we will be fit for the long winter."
"Yes," said Gerry, "the days are getting[8] shorter now. Soon we must find a nice cave[9] for our winter's sleep."
Larry crept further under his big rock. "I'm not going to ask these two big animals about the big wide river," he thought. "They look much too dangerous."

---

8 *to get* – werden
9 *cave* – Höhle

Chapter 20
Larry and the beaver

After the two grizzly bears had gone past, Larry felt[1] very tired. He made himself comfortable under the rock and was soon fast asleep.

***

He must have been very tired because the sun was already high in the sky, when he woke up. He yawned and licked his whiskers. "I must be on my way," he thought. He came out from under the big rock and ran along the river bank. After he had been running for some time, he heard a strange sound. It sounded[2] like someone cutting wood. He looked around and saw a funny creature[3] with a big flat tail gnawing[4] at a tree. He crept over and sat on the stump of another tree and watched. The other animal noticed him and said: "Who are you?"

"I'm Larry Lemming," replied our little friend.

---

1 *to feel, felt, felt* – sich fühlen
2 *to sound* – klingen
3 *creature* – Geschöpf
4 *to gnaw* – nagen

"Well, I wouldn't stay just there, Larry Lemming. One more nibble and this tree will fall on you." Larry looked up and saw the big tree towering[5] above him.

"Come here next to me," said the strange animal, "then you'll be safe." Larry ran quickly over and the animal started gnawing the tree again.

"Eeeeeek", went the tree and then, "craaash," as it hit the ground. The animal looked at Larry and smiled:

"Snip and snap, the trees taste good,
As my sharp teeth cut through the wood,
I choose the trees when they are tall;
The bigger they are, the nicer they fall."

***

5 *to tower* – sich auftürmen

"Heh, heh, heh," he snuffled, "that's another tree for our house. By the way, my name's Billy and I'm a beaver[6]." Then he started to gnaw at another tree.

"Is this the big wide river my father told me about?" asked Larry.

"That, I don't know," replied Billy, "but when we beavers build our houses, we change the small streams into wide rivers and lakes. Run down to the bank[7] and have a closer look." As Larry ran off, Billy Beaver called after him: "Heh, heh, heh, and watch out for falling trees."

---

6 *beaver* – Biber
7 *bank* – Ufer

Chapter 21
Larry makes a big decision

Larry ran down to the river bank between the stumps of trees. Near the bank, he saw another beaver pulling a big branch to the water. Larry saw that the beavers had made a dam across the river and behind it the river was very, very wide.

Suddenly he heard "plop", "plop", "plop" from along the bank. He saw that hundreds of other lemmings were coming down to the lake, too. So, "plop", Larry dived in and started swimming, too.

About half way across he swam past another lemming. "Help," cried a voice, "I'm getting tired. I can't swim much further[1]." Larry saw that it was Lotty the nice young lady lemming. "Keep swimming[2]," he told her, "you'll make it. I'll swim in front and you hold on to my tail."

Larry swam and swam, pulling little Lotty behind him. But the river was very, very wide and, when they reached the other bank, two very tired lemmings crawled out of the water.

***

When they had recovered[3], Larry said to Lotty: "I think that must be the big wide river our fathers told us about. Now I'm going to look for a nice place to make a nest for the winter. Would you like to come with me?" "Oh, yes," she answered, "we can build it together." So off ran Larry with Lotty following close[4] behind him.

They were going now to new lemming country. They were going to where there was lots of space and plenty of nice tasty roots and berries[5]. They were going to where it is very cold in winter and the snow is very deep. They were going to where most of the animals and birds wear white winter coats.

---

1 *further* – weiter
2 *keep swimming* – schwimm weiter
3 *to recover* – sich erholen
4 *close* – nahe
5 *berry* – Beere

***

I wonder[6] what more marvellous adventures they will have before they get there? I'm sure they will tell their own children many wonderful stories about those adventures. But I'm sure the first thing that they will tell them is: "Watch out, my little dears, for the black shadow!"

Larry has had such fine adventures,
He has found a nice new friend.
And now, like all good stories
We've come to a happy end.

6 *to wonder* – gespannt sein

(Bitte blättern Sie um)

Englisch Grundwissen

Englisch Grundwissen 5. Klasse ...... Best.-Nr. 90505
Englisch Grundwissen 6. Klasse ...... Best.-Nr. 90506
Englisch Grundwissen 7. Klasse ...... Best.-Nr. 90507
Englisch Grundwissen 8. Klasse ...... Best.-Nr. 90508
Englisch Grundwissen 9. Klasse ...... Best.-Nr. 90509
Englisch Grundwissen 10. Klasse .... Best.-Nr. 90510
Englisch Übertritt in die Oberstufe .. Best.-Nr. 82453
Kompakt-Wissen Kurzgrammatik .... Best.-Nr. 90461

Englisch Klassenarbeiten

Klassenarbeiten Englisch
5. Klasse mit CD .... Best.-Nr. 905053
Klassenarbeiten Englisch
6. Klasse mit CD .... Best.-Nr. 905063
Klassenarbeiten Englisch
7. Klasse mit CD .... Best.-Nr. 905073

Englisch Textproduktion

Textproduktion 9./10. Klasse .... Best.-Nr. 90541

Englisch Leseverstehen

Leseverstehen 5. Klasse .... Best.-Nr. 90526
Leseverstehen 6. Klasse .... Best.-Nr. 90525
Leseverstehen 8. Klasse .... Best.-Nr. 90522
Leseverstehen 10. Klasse .... Best.-Nr. 90521

Englisch Hörverstehen

Hörverstehen 5. Klasse mit CD .... Best.-Nr. 90512
Hörverstehen 6. Klasse mit CD .... Best.-Nr. 90511
Hörverstehen 7. Klasse mit CD .... Best.-Nr. 90513
Hörverstehen 9. Klasse mit CD .... Best.-Nr. 90515
Hörverstehen 10. Klasse mit CD ...... Best.-Nr. 80457

Englisch Rechtschreibung

Rechtschreibung und Diktat
5. Klasse mit 3 CDs .... Best.-Nr. 90531
Rechtschreibung und Diktat
6. Klasse mit CD .... Best.-Nr. 90532
Englische Rechtschreibung
9./10. Klasse .... Best.-Nr. 80453

Englisch Übersetzung

Translation Practice 1 / ab 9. Kl. .... Best.-Nr. 80451
Translation Practice 2 / ab 10. Kl. .... Best.-Nr. 80452

Englisch Wortschatzübung

Wortschatzübung 5. Klasse mit CD .. Best.-Nr. 90518
Wortschatzübung 6. Klasse mit CD .. Best.-Nr. 90519
Wortschatzübung Mittelstufe .... Best.-Nr. 90520
Kompakt-Wissen Grundwortschatz .. Best.-Nr. 90464

Englisch Lektüren

Alan Cartmell: *The Adventures of Larry Lemming*
Unterstufe .... Best.-Nr. 250030
Alan Cartmell: *Harry Hedgehog*
Unterstufe .... Best.-Nr. 250032
Alan Cartmell: *A Dog Called Leo*
Unterstufe .... Best.-Nr. 250033
Alan Cartmell: *The Green Feather*
Unterstufe .... Best.-Nr. 250034
Liam Cleary: *Echoes and Other Short Stories*
Mittelstufe .... Best.-Nr. 250008
Rainer Jacob: *Abenteuergeschichten 1*
Mittelstufe .... Best.-Nr. 80454

Geschichte

Kompakt-Wissen Geschichte
Unter-/Mittelstufe .... Best.-Nr. 907601

Chemie

Chemie – Mittelstufe 1 .... Best.-Nr. 90731

Ratgeber „Richtig Lernen"

Tipps und Lernstrategien
Unterstufe .... Best.-Nr. 10481
Tipps und Lernstrategien
Mittelstufe .... Best.-Nr. 10482

Bestellungen bitte direkt an:
STARK Verlagsgesellschaft mbH & Co. KG
Postfach 1852 · 85318 Freising
Tel: 0180 3 179000* · Fax: 0180 3 179001*
www.stark-verlag.de · info@stark-verlag.de
*9 Cent pro Min. aus dem deutschen Festnetz

Die echten Hilfen zum Lernen ...
STARK

17-V1M